This book is to be returned
the last date stamp

This Mammoth
belongs to

- - - - - - - - - - - - - - - - - - - - - - - - - -

- - - - - - - - - - - - - - - - - - - - - - - - - -

The kiss of the sun for pardon,
The song of the birds for mirth,
One is nearer God's heart in a garden
Than anywhere else on earth.

*Dorothy Frances Gurney*

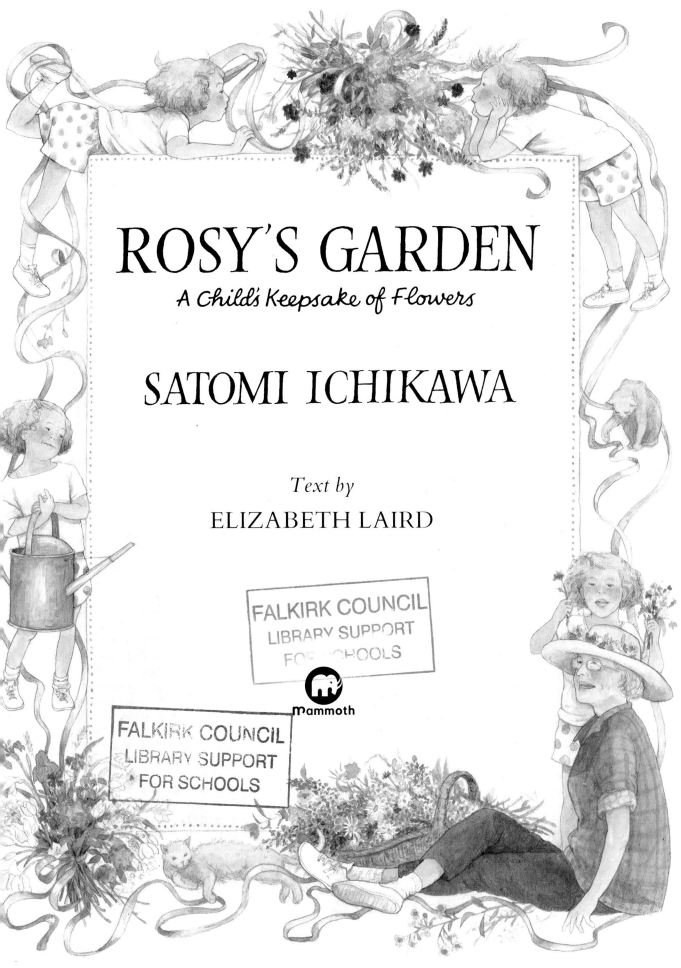

# ROSY'S GARDEN

*A Child's Keepsake of Flowers*

# SATOMI ICHIKAWA

*Text by*

# ELIZABETH LAIRD

mammoth

# A Welcome for Rosy

"Rosy!" says Granny happily. "You're here at last!"

Rosy skips into Granny's kitchen, and looks round. It's lovely – just as she remembers it. There are flowers everywhere, a jug of irises on the table, honeysuckle on the wallpaper, and Busy-Lizzie growing in pots on the window sill. There are other interesting things on the window sill too.

"What are those little plants?" says Rosy.

"More flowers," smiles Granny. "Pansies, and sweet williams, and petunias . . ."

"But there aren't any flowers on them," says Rosy.

"There will be soon," says Granny. "I'm going to plant them out in the garden tomorrow. Then they'll grow very fast."

"Can I help?" says Rosy. "I love gardening."

"Of course you can," says Granny. "You can be my Chief Assistant. I've got a special trowel and fork, just for you to use."

"But will the flowers come out before I have to go home?" says Rosy.

"Yes," says Granny. "Mother says you can stay for the whole summer if you want to."

"Oh, I do want to!" says Rosy, "I do!"

Then she notices something she has never seen before. Round Granny's neck is a locket. Rosy opens it. Inside are some little purple violets, rather faded, but still pretty.

"Where do these come from?" asks Rosy.

"It's a long story," says Granny. "Let me make myself a cup of tea, and I'll tell you all about it."

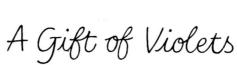

# A Gift of Violets

"My big brother Tom could run so fast, and climb so high, and scramble so quickly over fences that I could never catch up with him," Granny says. "Well, one lovely spring day, when I was six or seven years old, Mother said we could go into the woods to look for primroses, but when we got halfway there, Tom met his best friend. 'I've seen some baby thrushes in a nest,' he said. 'Come along, I'll show you.' Then they ran off, and left me all alone, in the woods!" said Granny.

"What did you do?" asks Rosy.

"I called out, and no one answered, so I sat down on a tree stump and cried."

"That's what I'd have done," says Rosy.

"But crying doesn't get you anywhere," says Granny, "so after a while I got up, and looked for a path, and at last I found my way home. The boys stayed out all day, looking for birds' nests. They even forgot to come home for tea."

"Was your mother cross?" asks Rosy.

"Yes," says Granny, "and so was I, but not for long, because the next day Tom's friend waited for me all morning in the garden, and when I came out in the afternoon, he gave me a bunch of violets, and said he was very sorry, and he'd never be horrid to me again."

"And was he?" says Rosy.

"No," says Granny. "Edward was the kindest man I ever knew."

"Edward?" says Rosy, "but that was Grandfather's name!"

"Yes, dear," says Granny, "and these are Edward's violets." And she carefully shuts the locket.

# Granny's Garden

Outside, in the garden, Rosy runs up
one path and down another.

"It's perfect!" she says. "It's the most
lovely garden I've ever seen! It's the
loveliest garden in the world!"

# Old Names for Old Flowers

"I wish I knew what all the flowers are called," says Rosy.

"You'll soon learn their names," says Granny, "and very ancient some of them are too. Some are even in a poem that's nearly six hundred years old.

> Periwinkle, violet, cowslip and lily,
> Rose red, rose white, foxglove and pimpernel,
> Hollyhock, coriander, peony . . ."

"It doesn't really sound like a poem," says Rosy. "It doesn't rhyme."

"No, it doesn't," says Granny. "You'd better make up another one when you know all the flower names yourself."

## CARNATION

These flowers were greatly loved in the Middle Ages. They were often used to make garlands and coronets, and came to be called 'coronation', or 'carnation'.

## LILY

Old painters loved this flower and often painted the Virgin Mary with lilies, so that it became the symbol of all that is good and beautiful.

## DELPHINIUM

The Greeks thought the buds of this flower looked like dolphins so they called it 'delphinos', which is Greek for dolphin. Delphinium comes from 'delphinos'.

## HOLLYHOCK

The Crusaders probably brought this flower to Europe from its home in the East. They used to make the flowers into a kind of tea and drink it when they had a bad cold.

## POPPY

In the First World War, a Canadian poet, John McCrae, wrote a famous poem about the poppies that grew in the fields of Flanders, where many soldiers died. Soon people started wearing poppies in honour of fallen soldiers.

## HONEYSUCKLE

Perhaps it is the sweet smell of honeysuckle that makes it so romantic. There's an old superstition that if you bring honeysuckle into the house a wedding will follow.

# Lavender Blue, Lavender Green

Rosy runs down a little stone path and brushes against a grey-green bush with small blue flowers.

"I know this one!" she says. "It's lavender! I know a song about it, too."

"Go on then," says Granny. "Sing it to me."

> Lavender's blue, diddle diddle,
> Lavender's green;
> When I am king, diddle diddle,
> You shall be queen.
>
> Roses are red, diddle diddle,
> Violets are blue;
> Because you love me, diddle diddle,
> I will love you.
>
> Who told you so, diddle, diddle,
> Who told you so?
> 'Twas mine own heart, diddle, diddle,
> That told me so.

"I used to sing that when I was your age," says Granny.

"Did you really?"

"Yes," says Granny, "and I did something else too. I used to sew little muslin bags and fill them with dried lavender flowers, then I'd tuck them in with my handkerchieves and clothes. They made everything smell lovely."

"Let's pick some lavender flowers, Granny, so that I can make a bag and take it home."

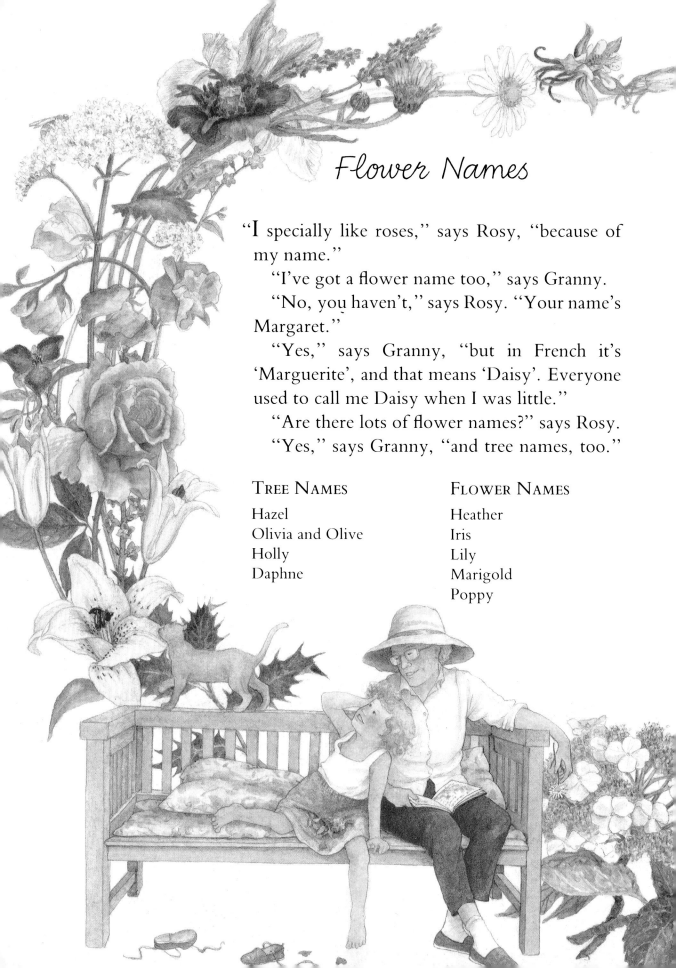

# Flower Names

"I specially like roses," says Rosy, "because of my name."

"I've got a flower name too," says Granny.

"No, you haven't," says Rosy. "Your name's Margaret."

"Yes," says Granny, "but in French it's 'Marguerite', and that means 'Daisy'. Everyone used to call me Daisy when I was little."

"Are there lots of flower names?" says Rosy.

"Yes," says Granny, "and tree names, too."

### TREE NAMES
Hazel
Olivia and Olive
Holly
Daphne

### FLOWER NAMES
Heather
Iris
Lily
Marigold
Poppy

# The Language of Flowers

"Did you know," says Granny, "that many flowers have a special meaning? In the old days, you had to be careful when you gave someone a posy of flowers. If they knew the language of flowers, they might think you were trying to give them a secret message. Red chrysanthemums meant 'I love', and four-leaved clover meant 'Be mine'. But hydrangeas meant 'Heartless' and Michaelmas daisies meant 'Goodbye'."

## SOME FLOWER MEANINGS

Anemone – *forsaken*
Bluebell – *constancy*
Red carnation – *alas for my poor heart!*
Columbine – *folly*
Cowslip – *thoughtfulness*
Daisy – *innocence*
Forget-me-not – *true love*
French marigold – *jealousy*
Hyacinth – *sport, or game*
Lavender – *distrust*
Lily – *purity, sweetness*
Lily of the valley – *return of happiness*

Marigold – *grief*
Orange blossom – *purity, loveliness*
Pansy – *thoughts*
Rose – *love*
Rosemary – *remembrance*
Snowdrop – *hope*
Violet – *modesty*
Yew – *sorrow*

# Fairy Dreams

The summer days pass quickly in Granny's garden. Stiff lupin spikes are standing in the flower bed, and the rosebuds are beginning to open. Soon the air is full of the scent of honeysuckle. It comes from Rosy's favourite part of the garden, an old summer house in a sleepy corner, almost smothered with creamy, pale-yellow flowers. Rosy likes to come here with a book and an apple on hot, lazy afternoons, and hear the bees, and as she curls up in her favourite chair, she murmurs a little poem to herself.

Honeysuckle, twisting, climbing
Round and over, up and down.
Every flower a Sleeping Beauty
In a lacy dressing gown.

Honeysuckle, heavy-scented,
On a lazy summer's day,
Yawning, nodding, eyelids closing,
Dreaming quiet hours away.

And when Rosy is fast asleep, who knows what little visitors might come and play around her?

# The Herb Garden

There's a corner of Granny's garden where only
herbs are allowed to grow. Rosy knows all their names.
"Rosemary, thyme, mint, parsley, sage . . ." she says, as she picks
a leaf off each plant and crushes them in her fingers. The rich, herby
smells make her think of times long ago, when medieval ladies
grew herbs in between neat little paths in the castle gardens, and
strewed herbs on the floor to make the great hall smell sweet, and
when they made medicines and ointments out of herbs, to cure
everything from headaches to bee-stings.

And where the marjoram once, and sage
    and rue
And balm and mint, with curled-leaved
    parsley grew,
And double marigold, and silver thyme,
And pumpkins 'neath the window used
    to climb;
And where I often, when a child, for hours,
Tried through the pales to get the tempting
    flowers.

*John Clare*

*pales – wooden fence*

# Herby Things

Granny knows lots of interesting things to do with herbs. She and Rosy try some of them out together.

## A HERBAL BATH

Chop up a cupful of rosemary leaves and lavender leaves. Put them in a saucepan and cover with a pint of water. Cover, bring to the boil, and simmer for thirty minutes. Leave to cool, keeping the lid of the saucepan on so that the smell does not escape. Strain into a jar and keep it in the bathroom. Add a cupful of the liquid to make a refreshing, sweet-smelling bath.

## A HERBY SANDWICH

*brown bread or roll*
*cream cheese*
*chives, mint and parsley*

Chop together chives, mint and parsley, mix well with the cream cheese and spread it on your bread or roll to make a delicious sandwich.

## A MINTY SALAD

*half a cucumber*
*a pint of yoghurt*
*half a cup of chopped mint*

Chop up the cucumber and stir in the yoghurt and mint. This makes a lovely cool salad on a hot day.

HERBY RICE
*8 oz long grain rice*
*1 pint of water*
*a knob of butter*
*a few slices of onion*
*a cupful of chopped herbs, parsley,*
*mint, thyme, marjoram*

Boil the rice and water together until the water has all disappeared, and the grains of rice are soft and fluffy (about 15 minutes). Stir in the butter, and onion chopped very small, and the herbs. This goes very well with any meat or fish dish.

# The Wild Flowers of Summer

At the bottom of Granny's garden a stream runs through a
meadow, bright with summer flowers. Buttercups and daisies,
meadowsweet and clover, ladies' smocks and dandelions all
grow there. The smallest flowers are the loveliest of all,
sky-blue speedwell, star-like scarlet pimpernel,
and yellow birds' foot trefoil.

# Flowery Games

Rosy picks a dandelion clock and blows on it. After four puffs all the seeds have blown away.

"It must be four o'clock," says Rosy.

"Nearly tea-time," says Granny.

She picks a buttercup and holds it under Rosy's chin. Her skin shines golden yellow.

"You *do* like butter," she says. "I thought so."

Rosy picks a daisy and pulls off the petals one by one.

"She loves me, she loves me not, she loves me," she says.

In the end, only one petal is left.

"She loves me!" says Rosy.

"Who does?" asks Granny.

"You do," says Rosy, and she skips off down the path.

"Pick me some more flowers," says Granny, "and I'll show you what we can do with them."

Rosy has picked a dandelion, a daisy, and a speedwell. She presses
them between sheets of newspaper and leaves them under a stack of
heavy books. In a week or two they'll be dry and flat, and Rosy will
be able to use them. She'll stick one at the top of a letter to Mother.

"Let's make some lavender notepaper," says Granny.
"It smells lovely. Then when you write to Mother, she'll
be able to smell the garden herself."

"How do you do it?" says Rosy.

"It's easy," says Granny.

LAVENDER NOTEPAPER

- CUT lavender heads just before the flowers open.
- TIE them in bunches and hang them away from the sun
  in a warm, dry, airy room.
- WHEN they are dry, shake off all the flowers.
- PUT handfuls of flowers into two or three envelopes,
  and seal them down.
- TUCK the envelopes among your notepaper.
- KEEP your notepaper in a box with a lid, so that
  the lavender smell does not waft away.

# Shy Flowers from the Alps

Granny's busy too. She's adding a few more embroidered flowers to Rosy's summer blouse. She does them in easy satin stitch in brightly-coloured silks.

Rosy looks like a little girl from the mountains in her embroidered blouse. It's covered in the bright little flowers that grow in the Alpine meadows. There are cornflowers, and jonquils, deep blue gentians, and the little white edelweiss, which once, so a Swiss legend says, was a beautiful maiden who died unmarried, and still lives on, high in the mountains, among the ice and snow, as a shy little flower.

# Seed-Time

It's late summer now, but Granny and Rosy still have plenty of work to do. They've collected a lot of seeds, and now they carefully store them in envelopes, ready to plant next year.

"How will they know when to start growing?" says Rosy.

"That's one of nature's secrets," says Granny. "The more you know about old Mother Nature, the more you see how wonderful she is."

# A Last Bouquet

It's Rosy's last morning in the country, and she's got a surprise for Granny.

"Do you remember that poem," she says, "the old one about flowers that didn't really rhyme? Well, I've made up another one.

> Larkspur and honeysuckle
> Candytuft and rose,
> In Granny's garden
> Everything grows.
>
> Hollyhock, lavender,
> Snapdragon too,
> Rosemary, thyme
> And forget-me-not blue.'

"Well done!" says Granny.
"There's a bit more," says Rosy.

> "Please Granny, please Granny,
> Please Granny dear,
> Please may I, please may I
> Come back next year?"

"Of course you can," says Granny, "but before you go home, there's one last job to do. Let's pick a bouquet of all the nicest flowers we can find for Mother. Are you ready, Chief Assistant?"

First published in Great Britain 1990
by William Heinemann Ltd
Published 1997 by Mammoth
an imprint of Reed International Books Ltd.
Michelin House, 81 Fulham Road, London SW3 6RB
and Auckland, Melbourne, Singapore and Toronto

10 9 8 7 6 5 4 3 2 1

Text copyright © Elizabeth Laird 1990
Illustrations copyright © Satomi Ichikawa 1990
The author and illustrator have asserted their moral rights

ISBN 0 7497 2869 8

A CIP catalogue record for this title
is available from the British Library

Produced by Mandarin Offset Ltd
Printed and bound in China